We request the honor of your presence
in playing

The Creativity Game

What: A Goal-Directed Problem-Solving-
Process

Why: To Develop Skills For Meeting Life's
Challenges In A Self-Satisfying Way

When: At Your Own Pace

How: One Step At A Time

Where: In The Magic Of Your Mind

Cynthia D. Bayern, Ph.D.
Diane E. Kramer, Ph.D.

Contents

With thanks to Rachel, Hank, Estelle, Steven, Shawn, Justin, Melissa and Florence.

Special thanks to Ang and the Candlelight Diner in Commack, New York.

And finally, with thanks to each other.

The Authors

CHAPTER ONE

Come Play the Game

Ready, Set...

Welcome to the Creativity Game! Playing this metaphorical life game will afford the opportunity to develop creative-problem-solving skills to use in designing a more meaningful and balanced life. Those who have practiced the **Creativity Game** process have improved their ability to move from life's "problem" spaces to "desired" spaces along innovative and satisfying pathways. They have internalized a set of "mental short-cuts" allowing them to achieve a balance of positive outcomes in different areas of their lives, including their relationships, work situations, and their mental and physical health.

Being creative can be defined as the process of combining old ideas or elements in new ways. Typically, being creative has been associated with generating products such as technological inventions, scientific theories, poems, paintings, and musical scores. The same creative process used to produce these tangibles can also be employed to generate personal resources, self-development skills, and effective coping strategies.

Those skilled in the **Creativity Game** process have reported using these problem-solving strategies to generate such wide-ranging resources as more self-confidence, assertiveness, new ways of organizing themselves, controlling their diet, developing a circle of friends, winning an election, and writing a book on creativity! One creative-problem-solver used the process to develop a public broadcasting television series investigating the effects of television on the quality of peoples' lives. With practice in creativity skills, resources can be generated to facilitate reaching most desired personal goals.

In addition to achieving personal goals, frequent use of creative-problem-solving strategies can lead to solutions for major challenges confronting our rapidly changing global society. The nuclear struggle, environmental deterioration, world-wide economic problems, nuclear family breakdown, the computer revolution, and the dawning of the age of robotics, make it important that everyone develop expertise and flexibility in creative-problem-solving simply to survive.

Steps of the Creativity Game

Becoming an expert player requires a steady and committed effort. The more you practice the game's steps, the more likely you are to produce creative solutions.

The six major steps on the way to solution are:

1. Constructing the Problem's Solution

2. Committing to Problem Solving

3. Commencing Problem Scrutiny

4. Conducting Possibilities Search

5. Choosing the Prime Solution

6. Carrying out Plan Systematically

(The frequently-used abbreviation for the general Creative-Problem-Solving Model is CPS. In the **Creativity Game** version of the Creative-Problem-Solving Model, each step of the process also has a CPS abbreviation to facilitate remembering the process.)

Following, each CPS step is defined briefly as a preview to its corresponding chapter:

CPS Step 1:   *Constructing the Problem's Solution* involves envisioning and clarifying what you want to create in life. Do you want to improve your primary relationship? Start a new business? Change your communication patterns? Take the **LIFE AREAS QUESTIONNAIRE** in the next chapter to discover new areas for your creative growth.

CPS Step 2: *Committing to Problem Solving* involves deciding to make a continuous committed effort to achieving desired life goals. Fill out the **LIFE DESIGN GRID** in Chapter **3** to facilitate perseverance in pursuit of your major life outcomes.

CPS Step 3: *Commencing Problem Scrutiny* involves perceiving and analyzing the various components of the problem and gathering information about it. GRASP* investigative processes to promote a full clarification of the problem situation.

CPS Step 4: *Conducting Possibilities Search* involves producing a multitude of possible alternatives which might eventually lead to solution. FIND IDEAS* to generate choices for a more satisfying life.

CPS Step 5: *Choosing the Prime Solution* involves determining which particular alternative(s) from all options offered, appear to be the best for solution. BEST PICKS* will facilitate effective decision making.

CPS Step 6: *Carrying out Plan Systematically* involves implementing the selected alternative(s) to reach the desired outcome CREACTION* is a format to organize an action plan to assist in implementation.

---

*These acronyms represent problem-solving strategies you will encounter in Chapters 4-7 respectively.

Frequent use of the **Creativity Game** process leads to increased awareness of each of the CPS steps in all areas of life. Becoming more aware of the steps leads to players becoming more decisive in their mental choice-points and eventually more skillful in ways of proceeding to solution.

Rules

The more the rules of the game are followed, the easier it becomes to advance through each CPS step and make transitions between steps. The general rules are:

- *Commit Yourself* to playing the game to reach a solution. This involves accepting the problem and practicing the steps required for solution-development. A considerable degree of self-discipline is necessary to get oneself moving and to keep the goal(s) firmly in mind.
- *Be Flexible* in choosing to explore different routes, rather than following previous patterns used to problem solve. Flexibility involves keeping open to new possibilities, i.e., not "getting stuck" in a problem space.
- *Compete Cooperatively* when you play. The life experience of many individuals suggests that solutions are reached more easily and enjoyably when *everybody* wins.
- *Enjoy Yourself* while you play the game! Learning to develop your personal strengths and resources is an exhilarating and positive force making participation in the game a valuable, productive, and fun experience. The "means to the end" can be as much fun as reaching the end goal itself.

Types of Players

Each problem-solver has his or her own way of meeting life's challenges. Many types of players have participated in the **Creativity Game.** Some, through practice, have developed the mental routines and the creative skills to solve their problems effectively. Others never get past "Start." Still others are continually getting blocked as they attempt to reach desired spaces or goals. See if you can recognize any of these life players, as a closer look is taken at their problem-solving styles.

- *The Expert*
  The Expert welcomes many problems and challenges into his or her life. He/she knows that life is about solving problems. Therefore, the more challenges are met and the more problems are solved, the more satisfaction will be experienced. The Expert sees problems from many viewpoints, is clear about the goals, moves through the problem-solving steps rapidly, uses intuitive knowledge effectively, and is able to suspend "critical judgment" until needed, so that many potential solutions can be generated. The expert problem-solver also knows it takes even more creative energy to implement an idea than to generate one. This person wins both ways in problem solving—while playing, and after reaching goal(s).

- *The Victim*
  The Victim feels deprived and unhappy. He/she sees other people playing the game well and making their lives work. The victim is perplexed about why he or she is not getting the desired results—not winning at the game. The past, the external world, chance, and even the unconscious are blamed for this deprivation. Frequent feelings include anxiety, depression, despair, and hopelessness. He or she gives up very early in the game.
  What separates the Victim from the Expert? It appears that the Victim has not learned to take responsibility for creating the "desired life" and believes there are "winners" and "losers," and that he or she is a "loser."

- *The Denier*
  The Denier rarely plays the game at all. He or she simply doesn't see many of the problems and challenges in life. When the unhappy spouse begins an affair, the Denier keeps smiling. When the bright daughter suddenly begins failing subjects in school, the Denier says, "She's only going through a stage!" When friends stop contacting him or her, this person says, "Oh, I'll make new friends later." He or she doesn't see new problems looming on the horizon until too late, because the Denier is so busy making "molehills out of mountains!" Underneath the smoothed-over exterior is usually found a core of inadequacy, apparently due to the fact that he or she has never developed the problem-solving resources needed to play the game well and make life work.

- *The Automaton*
  This player has a few habitual problem-solving strategies which are used over and over in different problem situations. When confronted with a problem, the Automaton tries to recall solutions which worked in the past for similar problems. Then, the first solution that comes to mind is settled upon. You can recognize Automatons by the extreme predictability of their responses. You can count on them to play the game by making the same old moves. The flaw in this problem-solving approach is that "when the going gets tough, this player can't get going" (due to lack of flexibility and minimal practice in playing the **Creativity Game**).

- *The Chaotic*
  The Chaotic player, while good at generating ideas, has no overall game plan. He or she tries to move in many different directions at the same time. When he or she moves, it is done in fits and starts, rather than in a smooth and flowing direction. Because of this disor-

ganized state, many of life's problems get worked on, but very few get worked out, i.e., this person rarely reaches desired spaces. In addition, the chaos of the mental habitat seems to prevent the chaotic player from recognizing the basic problem—this person has no overall structured process with which to organize his or her creativity.

Game Blocks

In football, the halfback's challenge is to run down the field, ball in hand, with hope of crossing the opponent's end line and scoring a touchdown. As he runs, he is confronted with the problem of how to avoid the tacklers attempting to block him and keep him from reaching his goal.

Similarly, in using the **Creativity Game** process, blocks will be coming at you at every turn. Some will be old friends—you've learned to deal with them successfully while problem solving in the past, and you know they don't present a threat now. Others will be like old enemies—they still present a threat to your attempts at problem-solving. Still others will be strangers—blocks you have not been aware of before, although they have always been there, stopping you from reaching your goals.

Throughout this book, you will learn many strategies for recognizing these blocks. You will also be offered many techniques for "unblocking" yourself. For now, see if you can recognize any of the blocks described below. Which are old friends? Old enemies? Which are you meeting for the first time?

- *Irrational Beliefs Block*
  Irrational beliefs are assumptions you have made about yourself which hinder you from reaching your goals. Common irrational beliefs include, "I can't change," "I'm not creative," "I'll change if he does," and "I was born this way." Included in this category may be irrational beliefs related to low self-esteem

and lack of self-confidence, such as, "I can't solve anything, I'm too stupid," or related to unrealistic expectations, such as, "If I can't master this challenge immediately, then I never will." Irrational beliefs keep you locked into self-defeating thought and action habits. Which are your most frequent irrational beliefs?

- *Anxiety State Blocks*
  Anxiety blocks involve states of internal disruption which keep you from taking the next step in problem-solving. With the proper techniques, such as relaxation, self-acceptance meditation, and listening to music, anxiety states can be overcome. However, because of the alarming nature of most anxiety states, players will often turn off the problem-solving path to avoid the anxiety experience. These "defensive" moves may make you feel better temporarily, but they only lead you farther from your goals. Are you aware of your anxiety states? What triggers them? How do you overcome them? What are your favorite defensive moves to avoid anxiety states?

- *Mental Set Blocks*
  Many times you may get stuck in habitual routes to solution without being aware of it. Routes taken too often sometimes become automatic. Generally, you may feel so comfortable with them, you may fail to recognize "short-cuts" to solution. Do you have any habits you'd like to change? Do you find you are in a "rut" in a particular life area?

- *Lack of Knowledge Blocks*
  Frequently, in moving toward solution, you can be blocked by a lack of knowledge about your problem. You may need new points of view and new strategies about how to proceed to solution. You may require use of additional sources of information (books, journals, magazines, experts in various fields) to help your progress through the creative process. Have you ever

experienced getting stuck because of a lack of knowledge about what to do for your next move?

- *External Blocks*
  Many times during problem solving, you meet external
  obstacles in the environment. You may feel blocked
  by the pressure of meeting deadlines, a missing part
  to a car that's being fixed, or having two important
  engagements to attend on the same evening. These
  types of obstacles often cause people to feel they
  are "victim" players, and consequently they get
  blocked from taking action and give up early in the
  problem-solving process. Do you find that certain external blocks recur during your routes to solution?

In the forthcoming chapters, you will learn many
strategies and techniques to overcome personal blocks
preventing you from moving more rapidly through the
pathways to solution. So, it's time to GET READY.... GET SET....
GO!

Now that you are aware of the general process, the
rules, the player types, and potential blocks, you are ready
to play the **Creativity Game**. Use the following exercises
as a pre-game warmup.

Warm-Up Exercises

1. List problems or challenges you may want to tackle in
   each of these different life areas:

Personal   *Family*

_____   _____

_____   _____

_____   _____

_____   _____

_____   _____
_____   _____
_____   _____
_____   _____
_____   _____

Community   *Global*

_____   _____
_____   _____
_____   _____
_____   _____
_____   _____
_____   _____
_____   _____
_____   _____

2. List the resources you think you need to meet your
   goals and solve your problems, e.g. a sense of humor,
   money:

_____   _____
_____   _____
_____   _____
_____   _____
_____   _____

_____   _____

_____   _____

_____   _____

_____   _____

3. List parts of yourself you would like to change to generate more life satisfaction: e.g. procrastination:

_____   _____

_____   _____

_____   _____

_____   _____

_____   _____

_____   _____

_____   _____

_____   _____

CHAPTER TWO

Envisioning: Constructing the Problem's Solution

> "We're sculptors of our own lives. We give ourselves a block of raw marble of great promise. We can spend our lifetime shaping and chipping and polishing it to make it an exquisite joyful work, or we can take a sledgehammer and smash the whole thing to pieces."
>
> Richard Bach (1984)

The goal for all who play the **Creativity Game** is to create a more satisfying life. What that satisfying life is like is just as individual as you are. In a few minutes, you will be invited to visit the Winner's Circle and *imagine* what that desired life might be like for you.

First, to fuel your imagination, let us share some life visions of highly creative-problem-solvers and illustrate how they moved from creation to action.

One creative individual wanted to see "caring" and "creative discovery" become mainstream teenage fads. To realize this vision, she contacted directors of commercial advertising agencies and suggested how to incorporate humanistic values and educational concepts into commercials. One person she contacted was the director of the company who produces the Calvin Klein jeans commercials. This player shared with the director her visions of a possible commercial—Brooke Shields comes out of a science lab, turns to her mother, and says she needs to buy two pair of jeans because hers wore out while preparing her project for the science fair!

Another individual, who envisioned more closeness and cooperation in her own family, developed a community workshop series called the "Family Creativity Olympics." Family members were trained in creative thinking and acting skills, and entire families worked in teams to solve problems presented at the Olympics. Problems included creating a family business, solving a who-dun-it mystery, and generating ways to improve the public school system. The goal of the Olympics was to serve as a model for family unity and to demonstrate that families can learn to enjoy working together in constructive ways.

Another creative person, Michael Murphy, psychologist/philosopher, and founder of Esalen Institute in California, had a vision about changing Soviet/American relations. He created the Soviet-American Relations Committee in 1982. Its purpose is to bring Americans and Russians closer together emotionally and spiritually, and to establish a kind of cultural bonding to help avert the dangers of nuclear war.

Yet another creative-problem-solver, Robert Muller, Assistant Secretary of the United Nations, had a clear vision of world peace. To implement this vision, he is developing both a United Nations College of World Peace and a World Core Curriculum. He hopes this World Core Curriculum, incorporating both world ecology information and humanistic values, will eventually be taught to everyone on earth.

Does Robert Muller's vision, and the others mentioned above, seem unrealistic? Are you a person with Robert Muller-type visions who believes they are unattainable? Herb Cohen, author of *You Can Negotiate Anything, (1980),* says, *"The trouble with people is not that they want too much but that they settle for too little."*

Limits

Why do people settle for too little? The answer is simple. Beginning in childhood they have *learned* to limit their thoughts, feelings, and actions to avoid disapproval from authority, to eliminate uncomfortable feelings, such as fear, connected with the unfamiliar, and to insure the acceptance of others. Once this limit-setting becomes habitual, people find it difficult to react to new situations in creative and adaptive ways. For example, one individual had an intense desire to play the piano as a child. His mother said a piano was too expensive. To avoid her disapproval, he gave up even thinking about what he wanted. It was only as an adult, through practicing the **Creativity Game,** that he rediscovered his lost dream, and bought a piano.

Another creative person, as a child, was repeatedly told, "Forget about it! You're fine!" whenever she was emotionally upset. These suggestions led her to avoid risky, challenging situations because she had not learned to deal with such emotional feelings as failure and disappointment. In practicing creative-problem-solving, she learned to experience and handle uncomfortable feelings, and went on to become a political leader in her community.

Are you aware of the "thinking, feeling, acting" limits you have set for yourself over the years? Accepted from others? To give you some hints about your true potential, list below some situations where your desires were blocked by these limits, then list the specific limits:

Situations	*Limits*
1. desire to play the piano as a child	1. mother says it's too expensive
2.	2.
3.	3.

4.	4.
5.	5.
6.	6.
7.	7.
8.	8.

Envisioning

Now that you have thought about some of your limits, perhaps reawakened some old dreams, and heard visions of other creative people, you are ready to create your life visions. To open the door of your imagination and allow new and satisfying life visions to emerge, follow these instructions:

1. Relax, sit quietly, and take some deep breaths.
2. Pretend that any blocks and limits have been removed.
3. Ask yourself, "What do I want in my life that is now missing?"
4. Take a few minutes and let your imagination create pictures, words, music, feelings about what you want.
5. Now ask yourself the four questions of creative self-discovery:

   - What do I need specifically in my life?
   - How much of it do I need?
   - When do I need it?
   - How do I know that I need it?

Allow yourself to play with this process for awhile. Having others help you elicit your responses is often very useful.

Continue the envisioning process by completing the following phrases:

1. Over the next ten years, my most important accomplish-

ments will be:

_____

_____

_____

_____

2. On the last day of my life, I will feel proud because:

_____

_____

_____

_____

3. Three new fields I'd like to learn about over my lifetime are:

_____

_____

_____

_____

4. By the year 2000, I'd like the world to have changed in the following ways:

_____

_____

_____

_____

5. This year, I can achieve more life satisfaction by:

_____

_____

_____

_____

6. Immediate changes I can make in my life to increase
   my life-satisfaction are:

_____

_____

_____

_____

While these exercises can be a start toward creating
new life visions, many creative problem solvers find they
need to keep updating their visions as circumstances
change. Holding to an initial vision or intention too rigidly
can be as disruptive to problem solving as not creating
the intention in the first place.

Life-Balance

Almost all life visions fall into three _CPS_ categories: _Connec-
tions, Productivity,_ and _Self-Health._ If an individual can
achieve balance in these three life areas (positive relationships, stimulating work situations, and mental and physical
health) life satisfaction can be maximized.

While many people are specialists in one life-satisfaction area, they are missing the creative skills necessary for
effective living in other areas. For example, one math-
ematician known to the authors, scores high in productivity,
as measured by salary, job title, and number of articles
published. However, she longs for a satisfying primary
relationship and smokes two packs of cigarettes a day.

In reviewing your life, do you maintain a positive _bal-
ance_ in the three life-satisfaction areas? In which life area(s)
do you need to use the **Creativity Game** process more

effectively? Below, a self-assessment tool is offered to help evaluate which particular life area situations you want to change. Completing the *Life Areas Questionnaire* along with envisioning your goals will prepare you for the next step—Commitment—in the **Creativity Game** process.

Life Areas Questionnaire
Connections (Relationships)

		Circle <u>Yes</u> <u>No</u>
1.	Do you have a satisfying balanced network of connections to fulfill your varied needs?	yes no
2.	Do you know how to make new connections?	yes no
3.	Do you know how to maintain healthy connections over time?	yes no yes no
4.	Is your connection time generally emotionally and mentally nourishing, encouraging your interests and goals?	yes no
5.	Do you know how to let go of unsatisfying connections?	yes no
6.	Do you know how to maintain your separateness, while staying connected, (by defining your "I" position, delivering messages about your needs, etc.)?	yes no
7.	Do you know how to deal effectively with an important connection (and with yourself), when this connection is being "critical", indifferent to you, or otherwise not satisfying your needs?	yes no
8.	Within your family, do you know how to be an effective parent, and an effective mate?	yes no

9. With your connections, do you know how   yes no
    to negotiate differences to mutually
    satisfying outcomes?

10. Do you know how to sense, and deal   yes no
    with, your own changing interpersonal
    needs (i.e. for closeness and distance,
    for giving and taking, for expression
    and control, etc.)?

Assign 1 point to each "yes" answer, and put the total
in the box below.

Connections = ☐

Productivity

1. Do you feel satisfied with your present   yes no
    career goal(s) or job(s)?

2. Do you feel excited and stimulated by a   yes no
    current project(s) on which you are
    working?

3. Do you feel you are progressing toward   yes no
    specific productivity goals?

4. Are you proud of your past   yes no
    accomplishments?

5. Do you have clearly defined long-term   yes no
    goals?

6. Do you know what steps need to be   yes no
    taken to reach your future goals,
    including how to influence others to
    meet these goals?

7. Do you feel like you're helping to   yes no
    produce the kind of world you (and your
    children) want to live in?

8.   Do you know how to move away from   yes no
      an unsatisfying work situation or vocation
      and redefine your goals?

9.   Are you aware of what attracts you in   yes no
      the world of productivity, aside from your
      own vocation?

10. Do you know how to find mentors and   yes no
      models in the world of productivity, and
      how to learn from them?

Assign 1 point to each "yes" answer, and put the total in the box below.

Productivity =   ☐

Self-Health

1.   Do you know how to sense your own   yes no
      emotional needs, and then find
      emotional support when needed?

2.   Do you know how to cope with and   yes no
      work through disappointments,
      tragedies, rejections, anger, and hurt?

3.   Do you know how to focus on the   yes no
      positive aspects of self (as opposed to
      the negative) and develop these
      aspects?

4.   Do you know how to use past   yes no
      failures and experiences as learnings
      in the present and for the future?

5.   Can you predict emotional upsets, and   yes no
      effectively deal with *transition* areas
      of life (career, marriage, deaths, illness?)

6. Can you separate your own wants   yes no
    and needs from others expectations
    of you?

7. Can you organize your time well enough   yes no
    to balance the various dimensions of
    your life?

8. Do you know how to identify "stressors"   yes no
    in your life, and then use problem-solving,
    stress-reduction and coping skills to
    deal with the "stress" effectively?

9. Do you take time to sense your short-   yes no
    term and long-term needs and then
    evaluate where you are at?

10. Can you effectively regulate your   yes no
    exercise, diet, and time-out for fun-
    and-relaxation needs?

Assign 1 point to each "yes" answer, and put the total in the box below.

Self-Health = [   ]

Now that you have completed the Life Areas Question-naire, plot your scores on the graph provided for you on the next page.

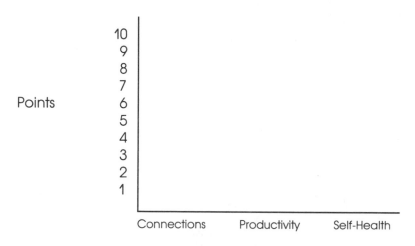

Points

Once you plot the three scores, simply connect the points to construct your current life-satisfaction graph. Use it as an overview for selecting challenges to work on while continuing through the **Creativity Game** process.

CHAPTER THREE

Commitment:
Committing to Problem Solving

Now that you have begun to envision a more satisfying life, you are ready to formulate a specific set of life visions and commit yourself to realizing them. Here you will create a "life design for life satisfaction" and internalize a set of commitment processes for actualizing your life plan.

Commitment is the second major step in the **Creativity Game** process. Without commitment, one is like an aimless sailboat, at the mercy of the winds. Through commitment to a set of life visions, one is likely to steer directly toward a desired destination. Staying on a committed course throughout the **Creativity Game** process is not easy. You must be willing to pay the price.

Pay the Price

Paying the price in the **Creativity Game** process means letting yourself be guided by a set of *Life Values* used by many experienced creative-problem-solvers.

Life Values

Left-Brain Values	Right-Brain Values
P erserverance	P layfulness
R esponsibility	R esourcefulness
I ntegrity	I magination
C ourage to create	C reativity
E xcellence	E xhilaration

The commitment to actualizing one's visions while being guided by these values generally leads to increased clarity of action, the achievement of life balance, and the flow of life satisfaction. To develop a heightened sensitivity to these Life Values, allow yourself to remember a time when you experienced each of these experiential states—e.g., when you had the *Courage to Create*, or *Imagination*. Once you have recalled a time for each state, ask yourself, "What would it be like if I experienced many of these states simultaneously?"

The Commitment Process

Before you commit yourself to developing a flow of life satisfaction that will be balanced in Connections, Productivity, and Self-Health, the Commitment Process in the **Creativity Game** requires you to discover what commitment means to you. To work through your ideas, answer the following questions.

1. What are your thoughts and feelings about commitment? Freely associate to the word "commitment" and list words or phrases that represent your thoughts and feelings: e.g. obligation _____   _____

_____   _____   _____

_____   _____   _____

_____   _____   _____

_____   _____   _____

2. Looking back on your life, review commitments you have made to yourself and others. List them below: *Commitments made and carried out—*

_____

_____

_____

_____

_____

Commitments made but not carried out—

_____

_____

_____

_____

3. Are you satisfied with the kind and level of past commitments you have made?

_____

Why do so many people have difficulty keeping their commitments? You, like many others, may experience commitment as "having to, but not wanting to," "a burden," "a chain around your neck." If this is so, you have probably internalized a set of societal expectations about how you "should" live your life. These expectations are dictated by institutions such as marriage, education, religion, and government. When the rules of these institutions hinder individual creative growth and development, people may react in a number of ways. They may feel burdened, depressed, and trapped and may enter into a state of "learned helplessness," thereby blocking any movement toward life satisfaction (Seligman, 1976). Or, they may choose to ignore commitments to societal expectations and simply live for the desires of the present, as the gambler who blows the rent money at the racetrack. Another reaction is to leave the institutions totally, as many adults have done by divorcing themselves from marriage. Another alternative is to place the needs of the system beyond personal needs, e.g., the "yes" man in an organization who loses touch with his own point of view. A fifth option is to "lash out against the system" to vent one's frustration and powerlessness, as by engaging in criminal actions. Last, one can try to change the system through social action, as in the anti-Vietnam War Movement and the Womens' Liberation Movement.

In contrast, experts of the **Creativity Game** problem-solving-process have discovered a formula. They have found that when what they Want to do (W) equals what they Have to do (H) and they are Committed (C) to this action, Life Satisfaction (LS) increases.

Well-balanced creative individuals who have discovered they love the foods which keep them healthy, have taken this formula to "heart". Well-balanced creative individuals who spend their vacation money and time attending educational workshops to enhance their social pleasures and professional productivity, have learned to keep this formula in "mind". Well-balanced creative individuals who devotedly commit themselves to serving the needs of others use this formula as their "soul" means of life satisfaction.

Having described different kinds of commitments, we now ask that you complete this phase of the commitment process by redefining your own personal meaning of commitment:

_____

_____

Life Design Grid

The first phase of the "commitment process" has been devoted to raising your awareness about definitions of commitment, assessing the kinds of commitments you have made in the past, and developing attitudes about future commitments. The next part of the "commitment process" requires you to choose specific *outcomes* for commitment.

To facilitate this phase, a **Life Design Grid** has been created where you can record your life satisfaction outcomes. The completed grid will serve as a guide toward the Winner's Circle and the realization of your visions. The more you continue to commit yourself to your outcomes, and the clearer they become over time, the more likely it is that your brain-mind-body system will select experiences which lead to the fulfillment of these outcomes.

Most people find that in the course of filling out the grid, it is helpful to differentiate *goals* from *outcomes*. Goals are general statements about what one wants, such as "I want to be rich." Outcomes are specific statements of what it will look, sound, and feel like when the goal is reached. For example, if the goal is to be rich ten years from now, one outcome might be to see your bankbook with a million dollars in it, hear people saying, "She did it," and feel tremendous pride and satisfaction.

In addition to defining specific outcomes, many well-balanced creative-problem-solvers find that the more their long- and short-term outcomes complement each other, the more chances exist for reaching these outcomes. These people have discovered that to achieve maximal life satisfaction, they need to move toward a balanced set of outcomes in many different life areas concurrently.

You are already familiar with the *CPS* life areas of *Connections, Productivity*, and *Self-Health*. These serve as the vertical headings of the **Life Design Grid.** The life areas composing the horizontal headings are the *Personal, Family, Community*, and *Global* dimensions. The combined matrix provides a balanced framework for recording a set of *outcomes* to lead to life satisfaction.

To assist you in filling out your own grid, we invite you to examine the completed **Life Design Grid** on the following page.

Life Design Grid

	Connections	Productivity	Self-Health
Personal	In two years, I intend to have a network of friends S** friendly faces H: the phone ringing with invitations F: warm, supportive closeness	In 1 year, I intend to complete a book S: my bank account doubled H: praise from media F: elation and completion	In 6 mos. I intend to lose 20 pounds S: fitting into a size 9 H: compliments F: light and energized
Family	I intend to take a family trip that all will enjoy S: new places and happy faces H: pleasant conversation F: love and cohesiveness	I intend to start a family business S: whole family working together in office H: customer reports of satisfaction F: proud	I intend to set up a family exercise program S: family bicycling in a park H: laughter F: healthy and physically fit
Community	I intend to organize a community picnic for fund-raising S: neighbors sharing food at the picnic H: neighbors discussing community issues F: pleased about community sharing	I intend to set up a community youth center S: children playing after school H: words of praise from parents and children F: security	I intend to set up a community health station S: neighbors getting blood pressure taken H: health information exchanges F: well-cared for
Global	I intend to create an international newsletter of community action S: newsletters mailed to many countries H: news of community action in other countries F: educated	I intend to set up international workshops to discuss the "nuclear race" S: myself talking in many countries H: ideas and opinions of others F: satisfaction in taking action	I intend to create stricter environmental controls S: myself lobbying at the U.N. H: support statements from others F: safe & purposeful

** S: — what you will *See* when your outcome is reached
   H: — what you will *Hear* when your outcome is reached
   F: — what you will *Feel* when your outcome is reached

Now it's your turn to fill in the **Life Design Grid** on the next page. Remember that your outcomes will most likely change and become more refined as you continue to become more familiar with the **Creativity Game** process. (The Appendix provides additional **Life Design Grids** for your later use.)

Here are some Outcome Questions to help guide you in selecting outcomes for your **Life Design Grid:**

1. What will you see, hear, feel when you experience the positive outcome?
2. What will happen in the rest of your life if you achieve your outcome?
3. What will change? What will stay the same?
4. What will be the negative payoff for getting your outcome? The positive payoff for not getting it?
5. Who will be affected by your achieving your outcome? How will they be affected?

Remember that an *outcome* is the result you want defined in terms of what it would look, sound, and feel like if you got what you wanted. An *outcome* works like a target. Set it up, relax, let go, and your brain-mind-body system will do the work of making a bullseye. The more you relax, let go, and become playful after you have set up your target, the more likely you are to reach it. So, fill out your own **Life Design Grid** and start committing yourself to aiming at your targets.

Staying Committed

Staying committed to your outcomes is a continuous rather than static process. It has been found that when subjects were given encouragement to continue to solution, halfway through a problem-solving task, solution or outcome-finding was increased significantly (Kramer & Bayern, 1984).

One way to stay committed to your outcomes is to review them often. A specific strategy is to write them on

Life Design Grid

	Connections	Productivity	Self-Health
Personal	S** H: F:	S: H: F:	S: H: F:
Family	S: H: F:	S: H: F:	S: H: F:
Community	S: H: F:	S: H: F:	S: H: F:
Global	S: H: F:	S: H: F:	S: H: F:

** S: – what you will *See* when your outcome is reached
   H: – what you will *Hear* when your outcome is reached
   F: – what you will *Feel* when your outcome is reached

index cards and look at them daily. This strategy also aids in revising your outcomes. Another strategy is to get support from peers and friends by telling them about your commitments. A third technique is to help those connected with you to reach their outcomes, i.e., you are more likely to get your results if you help others get theirs. This is referred to as a *Win-Win* situation. (Hint—to find out others' outcomes, ask them what they would see, hear, and feel if they reached their goal). A fourth strategy is to use the Envisioning process, as discussed in *Chapter Two*, and imagine your *Life Design* outcomes already achieved.

Perhaps you can add these strategies to those you already use and even create additional ones as you continue to be facilitated by the **Creativity Game** process.

Decommitting

This chapter has emphasized how to stay committed to specific outcomes. It is also important to develop a set of strategies for Decommitting from certain outcomes. When is it time to let go of a particular outcome?

One suggestion for a Decommitment strategy is to be in tune with any outcome in disharmony with the majority of your outcomes and to drop or modify it for a better fit. For example, persons who want to be tops in their field, have harmonious family relations, and be active community organizers, should think twice about sailing around the world alone for three years!

Another suggestion for Decommitting is to eliminate outcomes that are unrealistic, as a New York divorced individual with shared child custody who gives up her desire to live in California.

A third Decommitment strategy is to let go when you feel the process of reaching a desired outcome has become too painful, e.g., wanting to make an intimate relationhsip work, but experiencing a constant struggle for control.

We hope that by now you are committed to using the **Creativity Game** to define your visions or outcomes. As you continue through the steps in the problem-solving process, remember that the more outcomes you generate, the more likely your are to realize the ones most desirable for you. Are there current commitments you'd like to eliminate because they are too painful, too unrealistic, or out of harmony with the rest of your commitments? Once you have decided which visions you want to be committed to and which to eliminate, you can proceed to the next step in the **Creativity Game** and look more closely at what stands between you and your desired outcome, namely, the Problem Situation.

CHAPTER FOUR

Problem Analysis: Commence Problem Scrutiny

Now that you have completed the **Life Design Grid** and committed yourself to a balanced set of outcomes in the areas of Connections, Productivity, and Self-Health, you are ready for the Problem Analysis step of the **Creativity Game**. By the end of this step, you will have begun to internalize an expanded set of investigative skills to apply to your set of life challenges. You will know you have become a good "private investigator" when you can recall the basic processes of Problem Scrutiny, when you can identify applications of these basic processes in yourself and others, and finally when you can fully utilize the Problem Scrutiny processes while moving toward your balanced set of life outcomes.

Analyzing the Problem Situation in the **Creativity Game** means fully understanding what prevents reaching your outcome in a given area. For instance, imagine one of your outcomes is developing a support network of friends. In the Problem Analysis step of the **Creativity Game**, you may discover that you haven't developed adequate criteria for selecting friends who will support you. In listing criteria you may find that you would like to connect with people you can learn from and vice versa, people who listen and are really accepting, and people with whom you can have fun. The use of Problem Analysis skills will help you focus on your Problem Situation and determine what is blocking you from reaching your outcome.

Problem Analysis consists of five basic investigative processes:

1. Asking questions—formulating questions about the Problem-Situation.
2. Gathering information—collecting data about the Problem Situation.
3. Reduction of problem set—breaking the Problem Situation into component situations or subproblems.
4. Supraproblems—discovering the larger set of Problem Situations within which the current problem is embedded.
5. Perspective shifts—finding new perspectives from which to re-view and re-state the Problem Situation.

To facilitate recall of these Problem Analysis Processes, all you need is to get a good *GRASP* on yourself!

G athering information
R eduction of problem set
A sking questions
S upraproblems
P erspective shifts

Asking Questions

If you were to choose one symbol to represent mankind's highest achievements, what would it be? Karl Albrecht (1980), in *Brain Power,* chose this one—[?]. Children, in general, do what many adult creative-problem-solvers have to consciously practice for effective Problem Analysis—just "ask" as many questions as possible about the problem. By Asking Questions, the creative discovery process is put into operation to uncover previously unexplored possibilities. For example, this process was activated for Edward Land when his daughter, after being photographed one day, asked,

"Daddy, why can't I see the picture right now?" Inventively, this inquiry led him to develop the Polaroid Land Camera.

What kinds of questions best facilitate the creative-problem-solving process used in the **Creativity Game**? In addition to the standard "Why," "What," "When," "Who," "Where," and "How" curiosity questions many young children freely express, you can ask somewhat more structured questions to analyze your Problem Situation. Myers and Torrance (1965) suggest asking a question which taps into solutions you might consider improbable, namely, "What would happen if?" For example, in analyzing problems which may arise in our highly technological society, you might ask, "What would happen if all clocks stopped for a week?"

Many creative individuals use the "IWWMI" formula for analysis—"In what ways might I...?" Instead of posing a "Should I" question (which generally produces an either/or response—a "yes" or "no" alternative), asking "In what ways might I *do, decide, change, discover, accomplish,* what I really want?" will lead to a quantity of potential solutions. To practice this technique, imagine you have recently started a new business. You are heavily involved in administrative work, building up accounts and attending board meetings, all at the expense of your family. While establishing the business is very important to you, at the same time you feel you are not spending enough time with your family. To discover creative possibilities in this situation, pose questions about it in the exercise below.

Start your questions with "What might happen if" or "In what ways might I?"

_____

_____

_____

_____

Frequently the process of "re-questioning" our questions can be used to further Problem Analysis. In the exercise above, suppose you asked "What would happen if I worked a four-day week?" Re-questioning might lead you to ask a whole new series of questions from "How would this change my financial picture?" to "How can I do as much in four days as I used to do in five?"

Now go back and ask at least one question about each question you formulated in the above exercise:

_____

_____

_____

_____

_____

_____

_____

In addition to this type of questioning, here are specific problem questions many players find useful in facilitating Problem Analysis.

Problem Questions

1. What do you see, hear, feel, do when you are directly experiencing the Problem Situation?

2. What is the positive pay-off you get for *not* solving the problem?

3. Who else benefits by your not solving the problem?

4. Why haven't the solutions you tried in the past worked for this problem?

5. What is missing in the situation for you? What is needed?

6. What will be the positive and negative consequences of solving your problem and reaching your outcome?

7. Since you have not yet reached your outcome, is there a part of you which really doesn't want to reach outcome? What is that part doing for you and how does it work?

In asking these questions, one 180 lb. player who wanted to lose weight, discovered she was holding on to her weight due to a fear of dealing with men, as an attractive thin woman. This analysis led her to learn new ways of dealing with men, before she lost weight.

Using these suggestions, select one of your outcomes from the **Life Design Grid.** Try to flow with as many questions as possible in relation to this challenge.

State your outcome selection here:_____

Questions:_____

_____

_____

_____

_____

_____

_____

_____

_____

_____

Gathering Information

How will you find answers to the questions you posed about your Problem Situation in the previous section? The next step is to Gather Information. Being without information about a particular situation is like attempting to drive a car without gas. "Information fuel" is needed to keep the analysis going. Gathering Information insures that a wealth of possibilities will emerge in the forthcoming Idea-Generation stage.

The process of Gathering Information can be compared to wandering in pleasure and delight through a late spring flower garden, ablaze with blooms. You wander this way and that, stopping only to look closely at a certain flower here, a pattern of color there, and all the while smelling the fragrant mixture of changing perfumes, hearing the sounds of birds overhead and bees buzzing. You can do this for the sheer pleasure of the experience, or with an eye to Gathering Information to help create your own visually pleasing and sweet-smelling garden. This is the process of Gathering Information while engaged in creative Problem Analysis.

The innovative individual interested in introducing the creative discovery of ideas into mainstream advertising (mentioned in Chapter Two) followed this process of Gathering Information while analyzing her outcome. Her Information-Gathering method was based on a series of questions she formulated:

1. What are the current strategies behind commercials and how do they work to influence viewers?
2. What are the viewers' reactions to specific commercials?
3. If a commercial is a "turn off" to a viewer, what would the commercial have to be like for the viewer to be "turned on" to buying the product?
4. How does one create a commercial?
5. Who are the people to contact in the advertising field to create a difference in marketing?

With these questions in mind, the individual went into the world to Gather Information. For weeks, she noticed and discussed which commercials appealed to her and why. She recorded her ideas in her "Gathering Information" notebook. For instance, the Shearson/American Express "Minds-Over-Money" commercials appealed to her because she liked the multiple embedded meanings of the "Minds-Over-Money" slogan. Each day, she made sure to weave questions about commercials and their appeal, or lack of it, into conversations with the many people she encountered. One person she questioned about the "Minds-Over-Money" commercial said he was "turned off" by the background music, and never even noticed the different levels of the slogan. This opinion was food for thought. Again, she recorded all information in her notebook.

She also began to notice appealing colors, shapes and sounds. She compared these natural patterns to those she viewed in commercials. She gathered information about others' preferences for patterns as fuel for her future ideas of generating commercials.

At another level of observation, she questioned everyone she met about "what works" in terms of influencing the advertising fields. She kept her ears open to identify people within the system who create change—who can really make a difference.

To practice Information Gathering, spend some time thinking about how you currently Gather Information. Perhaps you already do a fine job in this area and have strategies which work well. Perhaps you would like to refine your strategies somewhat. In the space provided, write a few comments about what you already do to Gather Information.

_____

_____

_____

_____

_____

Now, refer to the selected outcome and the related questions you formulated in the Asking Questions section. To practice the Information Gathering process, see how much data you can collect about these questions.

Use information already stored in your memory, as well as any new observations you encounter. Record all information and observations.

_____

_____

_____

_____

_____

_____

_____

In future Problem Situations, remember, the more information you gather and the more questions you ask, the more easily you will reach a satisfying outcome. Developing the habit of recording questions and information about each problem will help you simultaneously move toward outcomes in a number of Life Areas.

Subproblems

Many individuals who tackle complex problems find that their goals are initially defined very broadly. For example, consider a person whose "Community" outcome is to improve the district's school system. Where does one start problem-solving here? One approach is to break the problem down into Subproblems. The breakdown analysis might include teacher training, hiring practices, teacher-student ratios, salaries, equipment, and parent participation. After the multitude of Subproblems are generated and Questioning and Information-Gathering strategies are applied to each Subproblem, specific target areas to work on to improve the school system can be chosen. As in the re-questioning technique of Problem Analysis, each Subproblem can be further divided into Sub-Subproblems.

To practice Subproblems, pretend you want to improve the educational system in your community. In the space below, list all the Subproblems you can think of:

_____

_____

_____

_____

_____

Next, consider the following family relations problem. The daughter in a family wants to marry a boy of a different race and her parents are opposed. List the Subproblems below:

e.g. acceptance by the community of this couple

_____

_____

_____

_____

Finally, continue with your selected outcome from the **Life Design Grid** used in the Question Asking section, and list as many Subproblems related to this outcome as you can:

_____

_____

_____

_____

_____

_____

Supraproblems

Many times, a problem is so embedded in a larger context of Problems-Supraproblems—that the presenting problem is difficult to solve without addressing the broader range of issues. An example is the widespread drug problem among adolescents. In analyzing the drug issue in any particular community, it becomes necessary to look at family relationships, community center and after school activities, employment opportunities, the level of human potential training in the area, pressures from the drugworld network to continue their profit-making operations, shared beliefs among peer groups, and availability of drug substitutes. All these issues need to be worked on to develop realistic solutions to the drug problem.

To practice looking at the broader range of issues related to the drug problem, list any other Supraproblems you can think of:

_____

_____

_____

_____

_____

_____

As a further exercise, list all interconnected world issues you can imagine which relate to world hunger:

_____

_____

_____

_____

_____

_____

Now, continue with the selected outcome from the **Life Design Grid** you have Asked Questions of, Gathered Information about, and listed Subproblems for. List as many Supraproblems as you can for this outcome:

_____

_____

_____

_____

_____

_____

Perspective Shifts

Getting a fresh perspective about a problem is like a light suddenly being turned on, a slide suddenly changing, or a channel being turned on television. These new perspectives or views fill one with a sense of brightness, hope, and wonder. They are part of the miracle of creative discovery. Whether one changes a viewpoint spontaneously, or is led to a new position by a series of exercises, one is always surprised and delighted by the breakthrough. Frequently, the Perspective Shift illuminates new ideas for solution and leads to successful outcomes.

Many times, because problems are looked at in the same old way, no hope for change or improvement is seen. For instance, one individual felt stuck in a relationship with his wife, which was characterized by a struggle for power. He felt hopeless about the situation, for a long time, until he began using techniques to develop some new perspectives about the situation. One tactic he used was *imaging*—he saw a picture of his wife in his mind's eye and stepped into her body. He imagined what it would feel like to be her. Using this strategy, he was able to discover what he was doing to provoke her and found ways to avoid these situations while still maintaining his own identity. This individual also could have developed Perspective Shifts by talking the situation over with his family and friends, putting himself into the shoes of outsiders to view his relationship with his wife as an observer, going away for awhile, putting the relationship on hold and focusing on himself, or imagining himself to be his wife's sister, priest, or dog!—anything to gain a fresh view. Finding ways to create new perspectives can be a delightful and fun-filled experience.

Another individual who experienced a Perspective Shift owned a small electronics firm. His problem was that his product market was invaded by a Japanese firm with which he could not compete. He was despondent, and walked around with a long face and drooping shoulders for months. One day, the light came back on, and he recognized that he didn't have to compete—his company would develop a new set of products. What blocked this person from seeing this new perspective sooner? Why was he stuck in viewing this problem in his old way for so long? We can only speculate—perhaps he had not internalized the Problem-Analysis shortcuts which may have allowed him to shift perspectives more rapidly and easily.

Select another person you consider highly involved in your Problem Situation and write a paragraph about what you think that person sees, hears, and feels about your problem and outcome. (If you can, when you are finished, show this paragraph to the person and see if he/she agrees with your interpretation.)

_____

_____

_____

_____

_____

_____

_____

_____

_____

Next use all your senses to facilitate development of new perspectives. In the space on the next page, make an abstract drawing of your Problem Situation on the left side, and another abstract drawing representing your desired outcome (what it will be like when you have achieved success) on the right. Below your drawings, list words or sounds that represent the pictures. Perhaps you would like to add some self-created poetry, or compose a little song about the pictures, or even do a spontaneous dance with movements that express the problem space, letting the movements flow into representing the desired outcome. Add similar creative representations of your own.

Problem State   Outcome State

By doing this exercise, you have begun to prepare your holistic brain-mind-body system to work effectively toward your outcome.

Problem Analyzed

Now that you have practiced analyzing one of your selected outcomes from the **Life Design Grid,** you can apply the Problem-Analysis process to all the outcomes recorded on your grid.

Hint: At any point in the **Creativity Game** process when you feel stuck and can't find a way to reach your outcome, return to the Problem-Analysis phase to recharge your batteries and gain forward momentum. In analyzing a situation, it is useful to pose a final analysis question to yourself. Ask yourself, "What is the *real* problem here?" and write a summary statement about what you discovered.

When you have *GRASPED* the essence of this chapter, you will have further expanded your set of strategies to expedite Problem Analysis. You will discover that the more you practice Problem-Analysis techniques, the more fun you will have and the more possibilities you will generate in the next step of problem-solving—the Idea-Generation step.

CHAPTER FIVE

Idea Generation:
Conduct Possibilities Search

Step into the mainstream of ideas, flow with the current of possibilities, and ride the rapids of choice. Experience the excitement of "letting go" to arrive at a sea of alternatives, submerging yourself in a body of potential solutions. The goal of this chapter is to offer techniques leading to the generation of ideas, which you can use as you move toward your life-satisfaction outcomes in the areas of Connections, Productivity, and Self-Health. In this stage of the **Creativity Game,** it is assumed that you have already created a balanced set of Life Design outcomes through envisioning, committed yourself to these outcomes, and analyzed the Problem Situation associated with achieving these desired states.

50 Ways to Leave Your Lover

"50 Ways to Leave Your Lover" written and recorded by Paul Simon,[1] is a song of ideas about a common problem—the problem of how to separate more easily from a loved one. Included might be situations such as when the relationship or marriage is over, when job relocation or travel causes physical distance, or when work schedules conflict. You may remember some of the extreme measures Paul Simon suggests in the chorus of the song which is reproduced on the next page...

---

[1]Lyrics Copyright © 1974 by Paul Simon. Used by permission.

Just slip out the back, Jack
Make a new plan, Stan
You don't need to be coy, Roy
Just get yourself free.

Hop on the bus, Gus
You don't need to discuss much
Just drop off the key, Lee
And get yourself free.[1]

While Simon's ideas about how to separate may not match yours, they open up interesting possibilities. Research has shown that the more possibilities that are generated for a specific problem, the more likely one is to arrive at an elegant and satisfying solution (Osborn, 1953). We invite you to use your imagination, flow with the problem of separating easily, and list as many ways as you can, temporarily or permanently, to "leave your lover." A few ideas have been listed to get you started.

Think about how to get as much as possible out of the relationship when you are together.

Realize that nothing lasts forever and take the positives of your previous relationship with you to the next one.

Plan for the next time the two of you will be together.

Take your loving feelings and learn to generalize them to the world.

_____

_____

_____

_____

_____

Now that you have generated possible solutions to the separation problem, scan your list and ask what method(s) you used to generate each one. Your answer(s) will provide information about your most prevalent Idea-Generating strategies. To add to your bag of Idea-Generating tricks, nine specific techniques are offered to help you to...

FIND IDEAS:

F orced Fit

I deastreaming

N etworking

D evelopment of humor

I dea groups

D ifferent modalities

E quilibrium / disequilibrium

A ssociations

S uperlearning

You will have the opportunity at the end of this chapter to apply each technique to specific outcomes from your **Life Design Grid.**

Forced Fit Techniques

The Forced Fit technique facilitates new ideas by creating a forced relationship between two or more normally unrelated products, ideas, or events, as the starting point for Idea Generation (Whiting, 1958). How can this technique be applied to produce ideas for "50 Ways to Leave Your Lover?"

One creative lover was faced with this challenge. How could she reduce the intensity of her feelings each time she and her lover temporarily separated? As she was driving home one evening after seeing him, she decided to use the Forced Fit technique by selecting, at random, an object from the surroundings to compare to her relationship. She chose the overhead parkway lights and began to generate similarities between their physical structure, patterning and qualities, and her relationship problem. Some ideas that occurred to her were:

• Just as the lighting poles were spaced in a regular fashion, so would the meetings with her lover continue.
• Even though there were dark spaces between the lights, there was enough light energy to keep her on track until reaching the next light (meeting).
• The sturdiness of the poles was compared to the durability of the relationship.

In this light, all the ideas she generated served to facilitate an easier separation (and, she became so involved in using the Forced Fit technique that she forgot about the painful feelings of "leaving her lover").

Ideastreaming

Many people are familiar with brainstorming, also known as Ideastreaming—a technique in which a solution is found by spontaneously producing a multitude of ideas while deferring judgment or evaluation of their worth. Group efforts in Ideastreaming are extremely productive since a suggestion from one group member can trigger an idea in another member. Osborn (1953) developed a basic set of four rules for effective brainstorming. First, no initial negative judgment of ideas is allowed; second, emphasis is on coming up with wild and bizarre ideas; third, quantity is desired; and finally, combinations and refinements of ideas already generated are encouraged. You have already had some practice with brainstorming or Ideastreaming when you generated possibilities for "50 Ways to Leave Your Lover."

Ways of getting started in Ideastreaming vary from individual to individual. Successful techniques in facilitating effective Ideastreaming are:

1. *Brainwriting*— One way creative-problem-solvers use this is by writing the problem or challenge in the middle of a piece of paper and allowing themselves to expand from the center by writing or drawing anything coming to mind until the paper is filled. Some use different colored pencils for categorizing different ideas related to their challenge.

2. *Physical Activity*—Some find that the faster their bodies move, the faster their minds move. These players jog, rollerskate, or swim to get a jump-start for their mind energy.

3. *Reviewing Problem-Analysis*—This technique is a trigger for brainstorming, in that reviewing the steps of problem scrutiny stimulates new and possible pathways for the Idea-Generation phase.

What triggered successful brainstorming for you in the past? Can you remember when your ideas flowed easily and how they felt?

Networking

Networks are group structures characterized by the mutual interconnectivity of their members. An illuminating example of how networking functions is *The Office of Open Network*,[2] an information and idea exchange that can be used by anyone for any purpose. This network is in the business of putting people in touch with others who share cooperative interests. For example, they received a letter from a man

---

[2]Founded by Lief Smith and Patricia Wagner, Directors, as cited in Grayson (1984).

in Singapore who needed information about computer data bases and set up a meeting for him with a regular network user, an information specialist, who happened to be going on a world trip and stopping in Singapore.

From time to time, use of a network of connections to generate ideas can be effective. One problem solver, when faced with a challenge, calls her friends for ideas. She keeps a file about which of her connections solved what kind of problem successfully, and uses it to guide her phone calls.

Another expert in the **Creativity Game** process, a nationally known family therapist, established her own international learning network. Each member has access to the system of 800 members whenever a problem arises.

A fourth creative idea generator collects ideas about getting ideas! She asks everyone she meets to describe their own methods of generating possibilities.

Development of Humor

Humor is a tonic, an elixir, a relaxant. How does it work in problem solving? A spoonful of humor gives a new view or perspective on the situation and clears the pathways for the discovery of ideas.

Successful users of the **Creativity Game** process attempt to find something humorous in any Problem Situation confronting them. Seeing the humor in a problematic situation is a way of reducing tension and gaining new perspectives.

Two prescriptions for lightening a Problem Situation and generating new possibilities through humor are:

1. Detach yourself from the intensity of the situation by imagining it as a child's game, figuring out what the next move is, and discovering how to have more fun while playing.

2. Try to create puns, metaphors, similes, analogies that

allow you to smile at your stressful situation. One player who borrowed a friend's favorite camera and accidentally broke it, eased his tension when he punned, "The thought of telling my friend about what happened to his camera makes me shutter!"

Idea Groups

One person using the **Creativity Game** started an Idea Group in the local library. The challenge was "How can we change our community into a model community?" He advertised in the local paper and found that many people attended the Idea Group meeting out of curiosity. Many stayed to establish an ongoing group to discuss the community situation.

Another way to approach Idea Grouping is to identify individuals whose qualities, traits, and processes are valuable for a particular type of problem, and assemble them into a group. For example, one creative individual was interested in generating solutions for world peace. She believed that individuals who had demonstrated excellence in skills such as influencing, high level creative-problem-solving, decision-making, global understanding, group facilitation, general systems knowledge, and making connections should be part of the **World Idea Group**. Each member need not possess all of these skills, but all must be committed to the outcome of a peaceful solution to the world megacrisis.

To develop your own Idea Group:
1. Identify your problem or challenge.
2. Identify individuals whose skills you think would be necessary to solve the problem.
3. Figure out a strategy for getting them to join your group.
4. Develop a strategy for continuing the Idea Group meetings.

Different Modalities

Using Different Modalities is a process in which all the senses are used in representing the Problem Situation and generating novel solutions.

One **Creativity Game** player had felt guilty when she didn't visit her mother every week. In playing with the problem, she converted her guilt feelings into different sensory modality representations by asking herself such questions as:

- What color are these feelings?
- What do they look like?
- How big are they?
- What characters from literature could she and her mother represent?

In the fantasy generated from answering these questions, she imaged herself as the 'whale' and her mother as 'Jonah.' She imagined the whale swallowing Jonah, symbolizing the reduction of her mother's power over her. Now, being in a position of power herself, the daughter was able to negotiate new rules for the relationship with her mother. Subsequently, the whale disgorged Jonah, representing a transformation in the mother-daughter relationship.

Vivid, detailed, and intense imagery is a powerful technique for Idea Generation. Many creativity tests tap into cross-modality creativity skills. For example, the *Sounds and Images Test* (Khatena & Torrance, 1981) requires subjects to think of images suggested by a series of sound effects. To practice imagery skills, every time you pick up a novel, read a newspaper or magazine, or listen to a song on the radio, try to colorfully image what you read and hear using all your sense modalities.

Equilibrium/Disequilibrium

To stimulate new ideas and thinking patterns, take a system—a family system, an individual system, a community system, or a global system—and try throwing it out of Equilibrium by creating some kind of unexpected change. For example, a professor who became disenchanted by the apathy and nonparticipation of his students, decided to throw his class into a state of Disequilibrium by announcing that, for the semester, he would teach only in response to questions raised by the students. During a given class period, at any point when questions stopped, he dismissed the class.

Natural causes, too, can throw a system into Disequilibrium. For instance, in one community where peaceful dullness reigned for years, a local beach cabana was blown away by a storm. This created a state of Disequilibrium for the usual system, as residents started battling with each other over the alleged owner of the cabana and his rights to rebuild. The issue led to deposing the local board of directors, rewriting the community by-laws, and eventually the building of a community cabana by volunteers. The scenario turned into a healing process leading to a new state of equilibrium.

Can you think of a specific relationship you are part of and a strategy for throwing it into Disequilibrium to generate new ideas for solution?

Associations

Association of ideas means linking one idea to another (idea-chaining). One easy application of the Association method for generating new ideas is writing down the first word you can think of which is related to your specific problem. Repeat the process by generating an Association to the first word, then to the second, until you have constructed a chain of connections. Reread your list and see if you can identify how the Associations were made. Try to make further Associations until new ideas begin to flow about the problem.

In facilitating ideas for problem-solving, associating past problems and solutions with current problems can be effective. For example, if you are intent upon achieving monetary success, you can start your Association process by linking up to a time in the past when you achieved excellence in a similar context. You may make word Associations about how you were motivated or influenced in the past, who else was involved, how you knew you were on the right track, and apply these Associations to your present situation.

Superlearning

Superlearning is a form of accelerated learning applied to the acquisition of factual data; the techniques of Superlearning involve both mind and body working together. According to Dr. Georgi Lozanov, the originator of the Superlearning method, the most effective way to learn rapidly is to be in a relaxed body state while breathing slowly and listening to music presented at a slow rate of 60 beats per minute. The material to be learned is verbally presented by an outside source and paced to the rhythm of the background music.

Reports of people remembering everything they see or hear, raising grades while shortening study hours, learning foreign languages in a matter of days, and excelling in any area because of new and powerful skills that foster good decision-making, have been documented through the application of Superlearning systems. For a complete course on Superlearning, refer to the step-by-step innovative techniques presented in the book *Superlearning* (Ostrander & Schroeder, 1970).

One superlearner, who uses these techniques every night before retiring, goes through the following routine:

- He does certain excercises and meditates, to relax and get oxygenated blood flowing to the brain.
- He listens to classical music with a 60 beat per minute

rhythm, while he fantasizes all aspects of his Problem Situation.

- He goes to sleep.
- He takes a brisk shower in the morning to get his blood flowing, and finds numerous ideas begin to pour out. (He keeps a waterproof pad and pen in the shower to prevent the ideas from "going down the drain!")

The prime underlying theory behind Superlearning is that when your logical mind, body, and creative mind are all working together in concert, you are in the best position to generate ideas and eventually make good decisions.

Applications of Idea-Generation Techniques to Your Life Design Outcomes

To facilitate the generation of ideas for more life satisfaction, an **Idea-Generation Chart** has been created for working on your *Life Design* outcomes. The sample chart on the next page contains three outcomes selected from the **Life Design Grid** in Chapter Three. The outcomes were selected from the personal areas of Connections, Productivity, and Self-Health and are: establishing a circle of friends, writing a book, and losing 20 pounds. For each of these outcomes, ideas have been generated using each of the *FIND IDEAS* techniques described in this chapter.

Choose any three outcomes from your own **Life Design Grid,** list them on page 60, and begin to *FIND IDEAS* using each Idea-Generating method. You can expect that the use of Idea-Generating methods will become more rapid and free-flowing with practice and experience in playing the **Creativity Game.** Once you become fluid in generating alternatives you will be ready to progress to the next step of the **Creativity Game** process—**Idea Selection.**

Idea-Generation Chart

	Circle of friends	Writing a book	Losing weight
Forced fit	steering wheel encourage your friends to share experiences so they become linked into a tight circle (as a steering wheel)	apple after eating an apple, the seeds are left, just as when the book is completed, seeds of information should be left for the reader	vacuum cleaner invent a harmless machine that sucks food out of the stomach after eating
Ideastreaming	ideastream criteria about what to look for in a friend	use a tape recorder in the car and record ideas for book while driving	ideastream substitute activities for eating
Networking	join *The Office for Open Network* to find friends	find partners to write with	connect with people who are trying to lose weight
Development of Humor	find a friend with a good sense of humor	write a funny story on the topic of your book	think of reasons why it's fun to be overweight (a la Erma Bombeck)
Idea Groups	form an idea group on "How to Choose Friends"	form a group based on the topic of your book	form a group diet plan
Different Modalities	hear the phone ringing with invitations to social activities	imagine the book you are working on already written and illustrated	picture yourself fitting into a size 9 dress
Equilibrium/ Disequilibrium	stop seeing your current friends to allow more time and motivation for developing new friendships	leave home for six months and write in a different setting	keep eating until you get sick
Associations	make associations for the word "friend"	read books related to your topic	make associations to overweight or expansive objects e.g., a balloon about to burst
Superlearning	learn the methods and offer a superlearning session for community people in your age range	do relaxation exercises and play Baroque music each time you sit down to write	do relaxation exercises when a stressful situation causes you to eat

Idea-Generation Chart

	Outcome 1	Outcome 2	Outcome 3
Forced fit (object)			
Ideastreaming			
Networking			
Development of Humor			
Idea Groups			
Different Modalities			
Equilibrium/ Disequilibrium			
Associations			
Superlearning			

CHAPTER SIX

Idea Selection:
Choose Prime Solution

Step up the ladder of creative-problem-solving to excellence in decision-making. Each rung will bring you closer to selecting the prime solution. When you've reached the top, you will have a clear view of the peak choice for future action.

If you are like most people, you are already satisfied with your Idea Selection processes in some life areas, and dissatisfied in others. For example, you may be satisfied with your vacation choices, but unhappy with your wardrobe selection for the trip. One creative individual, who has been married several times, always loves the lovers he chooses, but is perennially dissatisfied with the wives he selects. Another person, who teaches elementary school, is delighted with the summer travel time his job affords, but is disgusted with wise-cracking, gum-chewing sixth graders!

Accomplished practitioners of the **Creativity Game** find that by refining their Idea Selection (decision-making) strategies, they can increase the frequency of choosing effective solutions from among those generated in the Idea-Generation step. The result is that they experience a series of satisfying outcomes in many life areas simultaneously. Take a couple of experienced creative-problem-solvers who use the **Creativity Game** process to set up balanced satisfying lives. They have established a life routine in which they spend four days of the week together, and then pursue their careers and other relationships separately the other three days. Both their careers involve international traveling and marketing; they spend their time together refreshing and renewing their relationship as well as reworking their professional strategies and goals. They have decided to overcome feelings of jealousy and possessiveness and have developed a deep and loving commitment to each other. This couple has discovered that instead of making an excruciating choice between appetizing alternatives, they can "have their cake and eat it too."

To focus on Idea-Selection in the **Creativity Game** process and on the consequence of those selections, think about major decisions you have made in the areas of Connections, Productivity, and Self-Health. What strategies and steps have you used in making your decisions? What do you believe about the quality of your Idea-Selections? When making past choices, were you able to focus on the realistic long-term and short-term consequences of your choices?

To help focus on decisions you have made and their consequences, select five major decisions in the *Life Areas* and list them below:

Connections	Productivity	Self-Health
e.g. confronting your boss	e.g. changing careers	e.g. giving up a successful diet
_____	_____	_____
e.g. leaving home	e.g. going into business on your own	e.g. going for therapy
_____	_____	_____
1. _____	_____	_____
2. _____	_____	_____
3. _____	_____	_____

4. _____   _____   _____

5. _____   _____   _____

Now, based upon the consequences of these decisions, go back and rank order the decisions in each column from 1 to 5, 1 representing the best decision in the column and 5 representing the worst decision in the column. Think about your decisions. You probably know that some of them have turned out better than others. Is this a matter of chance, or is there a difference between the underlying strategies used in making successful versus unsuccessful decisions? The next section of this chapter will make you more aware of the steps and strategies involved in Idea Selection and decision-making.

Steps to Excellence in Idea Selection

Step 1. *Clarifying the Context*
Do you use the same strategies for decision-making regardless of context? For example, would you consider choosing a mate in the same way you would choose a meal? Consider the following decision-makers and the strategies they use in these two contexts, or problem areas:

Decision-maker 1 chooses to eat all of his meals at fast food chains, ignoring his own health and endangering his waistline. This person chooses his mates quickly and without forethought, ignoring his need for emotional nourishment. In other words, he uses the same strategies for decision-making in both contexts and is generally not pleased with the results.

On the other hand, decision-maker 2 follows a carefully designed diet plan, insuring a balanced daily intake of nutrients. In choosing a prime mate, he analyzes his long- and short-term needs in detail, and makes a selection only after a studied evaluation of mates in the running. While decision-maker 2, like decision-maker 1, uses the same strategies for both contexts, he is generally satisfied with his outcomes.

In contrast, decision-maker 3 uses one strategy for choosing a mate and another for choosing a meal. In ordering a meal, he asks himself, "What would appeal most to my appetite right now?", and selects on the basis of immediate feelings. In picking a mate, he carefully studies and prioritizes his criteria; he wants someone with whom he can share emotional nourishment, creativity, growth, commitment, and friendship. He develops very specific reality tests over time to differentiate the candidates. It is a long, thoughtful process and he is aware that it may take years to find the "right one."

By now, you may be reflecting on your own decision-making processes within various life-contexts. Do you believe your strategies match the context, or do you think you need to spend some 'awareness' time, realigning your decision-making strategies according to context? Do you need to develop new strategies? One person, in thinking about these questions, discovered that she was basing her mate selection on whether or not the potential mate "matched" a stored visual picture of what she wanted. No wonder her selections left much to be desired. With increased awareness, she was able to choose a better mate selection strategy. With practice in using the **Creativity Game** process, you will develop skills to facilitate matching context with appropriate decision-making strategies.

Step 2. *Establishing Criteria*

Within a given context or problem area, what criteria do you use as a basis for evaluating your alternatives? Are they clear enough so you can list them, or are they so vague and general that you don't know why you choose what you choose? People with vague and ineffective criteria often find themselves saying, "Now, why did I do that?" They are often unhappy with their choices and unclear about how they arrived at a given choice.

Confident decision-makers have found a basic technique to improve the decision-making process. They make their criteria explicit and then prioritize the criteria. For example, decision-maker 3 gathered information from people in successful relationships about their selection criteria. Based on this information and his own ideas, he carefully selected and prioritized his mate selection criteria, which eventually led to his entering into a satisfying primary relationship.

Step 3. *Weighing Importance*

Once you have developed your criteria within a given context, the next step is to evaluate the relative importance of a particular decision about your overall life satisfaction. For example, how important is your choice of a meal as compared to your choice of a mate? This extreme illustration clarifies the obvious point that some decisions need to be analyzed more carefully than others. Picture an obsessive-compulsive individual in a restaurant spending 30 agonizing minutes debating whether to order chicken cordon bleu or veal marsala. Contrast this with an expert creative-problem-solver who, upon being presented with many tempting specialities by the maitre d', focuses on the most important criterion for herself and says to him, "I want a chicken dish; bring me the one you think is best."

Step 4. *Representing the Alternatives*

In decision-making, it is important to represent fully in sensory awareness, the alternatives or choices involved, so they can be effectively evaluated. A full representation of an alternative would include how it looks, feels, sounds, tastes and smells. This representation process is necessary so decision-making strategies can operate on relevant choices. One individual, who was used to selecting a meal by only talking to himself about the alternatives, usually felt disappointed when he saw the food placed in front of him. To remedy this, he now makes complete sensory representations of his gustatory choices before ordering.

Being able to clearly envision the alternatives lifts one to a position where the different decision-making strategies can be applied to the array of possibilities.

Step 5. *Choosing Decision-Making Strategies*

Climb to Step 5 and survey Idea-Selection strategies for effective decision-making. A menu of strategies will now be offered. You should select the one(s) which best satisfy your appetite within a given context. The items on the menu represent the **BEST PICKS** in Idea-Selection strategies. They are:

B rain Grid

E valuating Criteria

S ubmodalities

T ime Frame

P rioritizing

I nformation Gathering

C onsequences

K ey Alternatives-Forced Choice

S ensory Modality Strategies

The Family-Productivity Outcome, from the **Life Design Grid**, has been selected as the example to illustrate *BEST PICKS* strategies. In this example, the specific family business to be developed is the organization of local creativity seminars.

After each descriptiion of a *BEST PICKS* strategy, practice space is provided. Choose a current decision you need to make and work it through, using the strategy. In the applications section following the description of the strategies, you will have the opportunity to select a family outcome from your own **Life Design Grid** and apply the steps and strategies of effective decision-making to that outcome.

Brain Grid

This decision-making strategy is similar to a technique suggested by David Loye in *The Sphinx and the Rainbow*. When using the **Brain Grid** strategy, first represent a current decision dilemma in a clear statement such as, "Should I locate the family business in a home office, or away from home?" Then fill in the Brain Grid as follows:

	Left	Right
Home Office		X
Away from Home Office	X	

In Phase 1, you ask the right side of your brain to provide a quick intuitive response to the decision dilemma, and then record the response in the correct box above. In this example, the intuitive right response is "home office."

In Phase 2, ask the left side of your brain to provide a logical response to the decision dilemma, by first listing the pros and cons of each alternative, prioritizing, and selecting the best alternative. In this example, the logical left response is "away from home office."

Now you are faced with another decision dilemma—left and right do not agree! When this happens, the wisdom is to suspend judgment, ask more questions, gather more information, and review the left-brain pros and cons until one side or the other shifts into agreement. Obviously, when left and right agree, a green light agreement (yes-yes) can be used as a signal to proceed with caution, and a red light agreement (no-no) can be used as a signal to consider coming to a complete halt.

Practice here, using a current decision dilemma.

Left	Right

Evaluating Criteria

This strategy is used in decision-making when criteria need to be established in a new choice-making area, and when criteria in an old context need to be updated. For example, in a new choice-making area, in deciding if a family business should be developed, one should devise criteria against which to evaluate the proposal. Criteria might include salaries, locale, disruption of family life, and use of personal skills.

In updating old criteria, the time to start is usually when one feels dissatisfied with a particular life area. In this circumstance, a reevaluation and expansion of old criteria can lead to better selection of possible alternatives. A familiar case involves a teacher who finds himself growing more and more dissatisfied because he is not able to use newly acquired skills on the job. He reevaluates his job criteria to include creative-problem-solving opportunities and organizational leadership, and decides to become director of a child guidance center.

Practice this strategy using one of your current decisions.

_____

_____

_____

_____

Submodalities

In the Submodalities decision-making strategy, remembered decisions are used to guide the current decision-making process. Specifically, mentally view a past excellent decision and a bad decision, as if you were watching a movie. Next, mark the qualities you notice in each movie on the **Submodalities Chart** on page 70. For instance, is the excellent decision movie in or out of focus? Is it bright or dim? In Column 3, note the main differences between the two movies. Finally, construct a mental movie representing the choices in your current decision dilemma, that is, whether to call the family business "Creative Locals Express" or "Creative Natives," making sure that the movie follows the form of the excellent decision movie viewed in the first step. The idea behind this strategy is that if you duplicate the form of a successful past decision, you may increase the possibility of making excellent current decisions.

Write down a successful decision that you have made in the past:

_____

_____

_____

Write down a non-successful decision that you have made in the past:

_____

_____

_____

Proceed to fill out the Submodalities Chart below and compare the sensory memories of these two decisions.

Submodalities Chart[3]

VISUAL	Successful Decision	Non-Successful	Difference
color			
black/white			
slide			
motion picture			
bright			
dark			
big			
small			
close			
far away			
clear			
fuzzy			
involved in it			
observing It			
dimensional			
flat			
fast			
slow			
AUDITORY			
loud			
soft			
sound			
words			
internal			

external			
near			
far			
high tone			
low tone			
fast tempo			
slow tempo			
continuous			
discontinuous			
whose voice?			
KINESTHETIC			
temperature?			
texture?			
pressure?			
movement?			
Smell?			
Taste?			

Time Frame

A helpful technique for decision-making is to set an arbitrary time limit for when the decision will be made and research the alternatives thoroughly before the deadline. For example, an arbitrary time limit for determining a site for family creativity seminars can be established, and if it is not selected by this deadline, the business will be developed at home.

In some cases, time limits are imposed naturally, forcing a selection from alternatives based upon expediency. In the family business example, a natural time limit might be imposed when a particular office space would only be on the market for the next month, forcing a decision within that time period.

As practice, set up a Time Frame including deadlines for some choices you need to make for the outcome on

---

[3]Adapted from a similar chart generated by Andre deZanger of deZanger Associates.

which you're working:

_____

_____

_____

_____

Prioritizing

Another strategy for selecting ideas is to review the range of possibilities and rank them in terms of which come closest to matching your most important criteria. To determine your most important criteria for a given problem or subproblem, ask what value each criterion has for you, and how urgent or essential it is. In the example of the family business of developing local creativity seminars, consider the subproblem of selecting an appropriate name for the organization. In choosing a name, it was decided that the important criteria in rank order, were that the name be catchy, easily remembered, representative of the organization, positive sounding, inspiring, and unique. In ranking possibilities against these important criteria, out of a range of many suggestions the name chosen was Alter-Natives, Inc.!

Practice: First, select criteria to evaluate the choice that you're considering for your outcome.
Next, prioritize the criteria.
Now evaluate the alternatives for your outcome against the prioritized criteria.

_____

_____

_____

_____

Information-Gathering

Information-gathering is a popular technique used in many steps of the **Creativity Game**, including Problem Analysis, Idea Generation, and Idea Selection. The reason for its popularity is that at any point in the process when a player experiences "getting stuck," Gathering Information may create a breakthrough.

In the family business example, there was much hesitation about the order of the action steps. No one in the family knew how to proceed. To facilitate their decision making, they consulted with others who had started their own family business. Once this information had been gathered, they were able to decide how to proceed.

To practice this technique, consult experts who have information about your outcome.

Consequences

An interesting technique for selecting ideas is to try them out ahead of time either by role-playing, visualizing, or temporarily living each choice, and then imagining the Consequences. In evaluating Consequences, consider what is positive or negative, and what is interesting about each alternative. For example, in deciding on a location for the business, family members can visualize the Consequences of developing the business at home: The negative Consequences include disruptions, clutter, lack of separation between personal and business time, and lack of social stimulation. On the other hand, in focusing on the positive Consequences, business at home insures that the children will be taken care of after school, costs will be minimized, and travel time will be reduced. The interesting consequence of going with a family business at home is that it offers family members a challenge to maintain a healthy balance between family and personal time and space.

Practice evaluating the Consequences on one of your current choices. List the positive and negative Consequences of each alternative:

_____

_____

_____

_____

Key Alternatives—Forced Choice

This technique is based on the process of elimination of choices. In Forced Choice of Key Alternatives, you compare two alternatives at a time, from the set of possible alternatives, and select one over the other based upon the important criteria. Continue this process until only one alternative is left. For example, in choosing a logo for the family business, 25 possibilities were generated. Using Forced Choice, family members systematically compared two at a time and selected one of the pair to be compared with the next selection on the list. The process continued until one logo remained.

Practice comparing Key Alternatives for your outcome:

_____

_____

_____

_____

Sensory Modalities

To increase the effectiveness of decision-making, many creative individuals do a Sensory Modalities check of their choices. In the case of developing a family business, members might choose between attending a series of "Creative Career Workshops," or taking courses on family business management. To aid in decision-making, each family member could conduct a sensory check of the alternatives. To do this, the person compares the alternatives to each other visually, and asks, "Which looks better?"; then gets a feeling about each alternative, and asks "Which feels better?"; and then, talks to himself about the alternatives, and asks, "Which sounds better?" He may continue the process using smell and taste. Many creative choice-makers who use this strategy discover that they can choose easily and quickly from a number of alternatives by making comparisons within each modality.

In considering this technique, the question often arises, "What happens if the visual modality check suggests one alternative as the best, but the auditory check suggests a different one as the best?" In such a case, it is often useful to go back and generate more choices. It may also be helpful to reevaluate criteria.

Practice comparing the choices for your outcome using the Sensory Modalities tests described above.

Application of Steps to Excellent Decision-Making to Your Life Design Outcomes

Now you can apply the Steps to Excellent Decision-Making, including *BEST PICKS*, to the specific Life Design outcome you generated in Chapter Two. Choose a family outcome to work through the process of Idea Selection and record it on the Idea-Selection chart on the next page. Attempt to complete the chart and to use different *BEST PICKS* strategies to facilitate your decision-making process.

Steps to Excellence in Decision-Making

Idea-Selection Chart

Family Outcome: _____
Specific decision
to be made about
the outcome: _____

Steps:

1. Context:
   (state the
   context of
   this decision)

2. Criteria:
   (list the
   relevant
   criteria)

3. Importance:
   (rate the
   importance of
   the decision to
   your life)

4. Decision Alternatives
   Set: (list possible
   choices from which the
   decision will be made)

5. Strategies:
   (list some of the BEST
   PICKS strategies you can
   use to clarify your
   decision selection)
   then apply them to
   the alternatives

6. Decision Reached:

To achieve any major life outcome, it is clear that many subproblems must be analyzed, and numerous sets of ideas generated. Multiple decisions need to be made in selecting the best alternatives from each idea set to prepare for the next step in the **Creativity Game** process —Implementation.

CHAPTER SEVEN

Idea Implementation: Carry Out Plan Systematically

You have moved through the Commitment step, the Analysis step, the Idea-Generation step, and the Idea-Selection step of the **Creativity Game**. Now it is time to move along the action pathway and carry out your plan in a systematic way.

To start along the action path, take one step at a time, overcoming obstacles as you go. Be alert for new approaches, detours, and sidetracks along the way. As you continue along the pathway, check your decision-making compass frequently and consult your problem-solving map to make sure you are headed in the right direction.

If you find yourself on the wrong path, return to where you went astray, and head out again. Make sure you enjoy the walk. It is a good idea to praise yourself along the way for making progress, for correcting errors, and for completing tasks. You may meet other creative-problem-solvers who can support and cooperate with you. For many, working with compatible others speeds up the Implementation step. When you ultimately reach the Winner's Circle, you will be ready to experience the satisfaction of having achieved your outcome in the areas of Connections, Productivity, and Self-Health.

Advancing obviously means you have envisioned your outcome, generated ideas for reaching the goal, and have decided which set of ideas will best fit the situation. If your outcome is simple, as making a cup of coffee, action is simple: follow the steps for brewing coffee and then "drink"—outcome achieved. On the other hand, if your outcome is more complex, such as entering into a primary relationship, you might need to spend more time in the planning phase of Implementation before continuing along the action path.

In this chapter on Implementation, many strategies will be discussed to help you "ease on down the road." To facilitate use of these strategies, they have been organized into a CREACTION PLAN:

C hunking
R isk Factor Analysis
E valuation
A ction Steps
C oncretizing
T iming
I nternalizing Obstacles
O vercoming Obstacles
N ecessity Thinking

To illustrate the use of these *Creaction* strategies, let's focus on an outcome from the **Life Design Grid**. This time the outcome is from the *Community-Productivity* Life Area —establishing a Community Youth Center. Each *Creaction* strategy will be applied to this outcome.

Chunking

Chunking is the process of dividing one's action plan into manageable units or chunks. George Miller (1956), a famous psychologist, states that most people can handle optimally seven chunks or units of information. In Chunking your action plan, an effective strategy is to write down all the component parts or units.

As an example, take a look at the Community-Productivity Outcome—developing a Community Youth Center. What might the possible chunks of such a program be?

Some of the possibilities are listed below. Brainstorm along with these suggestions and add any chunks which seem to be missing.

1. site
2. staff
3. fund-raising
4. overcoming community objections/ gaining community support
5. operations
6. planning and development

_____

_____

_____

_____

_____

_____

These are the most obvious chunks of information. To practice, choose a personal outcome for which you have already generated and selected ideas, and organize what needs to be implemented into six or seven clear chunks.

_____

_____

_____

_____

_____

_____

Risk Factor Analysis

What action steps might involve risks of failure? Can you reduce or eliminate these risks? Can you develop alternative plans? Even though you have decided to go ahead, it is impossible to control for all the external variables which might affect your outcome. Being aware of possible risks, however, helps eliminate some unnecessary moves.

One user of the **Creativity Game** process decided to seek a primary relationship, and formulated specific criteria for pursuing that outcome. She decided to find someone who could provide her with emotional nourishment, share her love of learning and creativity, be her best friend and share intimacies, and who could supply security and excitement.

Setting out along the action path to find this mate, she discovered a likely candidate. However, he wasn't interested in settling down. She decided to continue pursuing him, although the risk of rejection was high. Her strategy was to continue her pursuit while setting a time limit. If he was not more responsive by a certain deadline, she would switch outcomes.

In establishing a Community-Youth Center, one risk might be that participation by children in the community could be slight. In working on an action plan for one of your outcomes, be sure to analyze the risks involved in Implementation. Be prepared to switch plans if a risky move proves unfruitful. To practice Risk Analysis, choose an outcome you are currently seeking. Review and list the action steps you plan to take and note below the risks involved as well as alternate routes.

_____

_____

_____

_____

_____

_____

Evaluation

As you move down the action path, it is important to make frequent stops to evaluate your progress. An Evaluation strategy is to review your original outcome—review the Problem Analysis phase, review Idea Generation, Idea Selection and Implementation as well. In doing so, ask yourself questions such as "Is this outcome what I really want?" "Do I still want it?" 'Is it time to switch to another outcome?" "How will I know if I should switch outcomes?"

In reviewing the Problem Analysis phase, ask,, "Have I analyzed accurately?" "Is there any new information I need to analyze?"

In reviewing the Idea-Generation phase you can ask, "From this point in the action path, do I see any new ideas on the horizon to help me achieve my outcome?" "What might they be?"

Moving to the Idea-Selection phase, question if you still believe your decision is a good one. In the Implementation phase, ask, "What additional steps are needed, or can be eliminated to actualize my vision?"

In applying the Evaluation process to the Community Youth Center outcome, it was found that more data was necessary to assess community needs. New ideas for community projects needed to be generated and a feedback system for monitoring results had to be developed.

Think through one of your outcomes now. Does Evaluation reveal a need to change outcomes, modify plans, gather more information?

_____

_____

_____

_____

_____

Action Steps

This strategy is perhaps the most important for systematizing your action plan. To use this method, specify how many and what kinds of tasks are necessary for carrying out the selected decision.

It is a good idea to list all the tasks involved and rank them according to need and/or immediacy of action. Ask, "Which can be done right now to get started on the outcome and which can be done soon versus which will take some time to implement?" Ask, "Which can I set up immediately for future impact on the overall plan?" See if you can organize the steps so they will relate to each other in a specific time sequence.

In setting up a Community Youth Center, the Action Steps may be organized as follows:

1. Coordinating a board of directors to work on the project.
2. Assessing community need and support (sending out surveys).
3. Establishing a location.
4. Fund-Raising
5. Equipment and purchasing
6. Interviewing and hiring an instructional and supervisory staff.
7. Public relations.
8. Maintenance requirements.
9. Ongoing calendar of events and activities sponsored by the center.

Select a specific outcome of your own, and list the Action Steps to be taken for goal achievement.

_____

_____

_____

_____

Concretizing

The process of Concretizing involves taking each part of the *Creaction* plan and translating it into sensory specific language. Once this has happened, you will be clear about when each part of the plan has been completed.

Here are a few examples to make the point. In the section on Chunking, one chunk was finding staff to run the community center. You know you will achieve that result when applications for positions are on your desk! Another chunk was operations. You know you will have concretized this goal when you have a completed plan approved by the appropriate governmental agencies.

Concretizing can also be applied to other *Creaction* strategies. In the Evaluation strategy, you can concretize your evaluation by writing down your revised outcome and listing your new ideas.

A strategy for Concretizing is to review each step of the action plan for a particular outcome, and ask, "How will I know that this task has been accomplished?" Try to concretize each Action Step listed in the previous exercise.

_____

_____

_____

_____

Timing

A basic technique for proceeding with your plan is to for-mulate a Timing schedule. To use this successfully, it is helpful to review your Action Steps and determine how much time it would take to complete each one. Take into account the time allotted for the project as well as how much time you and others involved can give to related projects. (This analysis should be diligent and reasonable, since many people tend to underestimate the time needed for their plans.)

In setting up a Community Youth Center, one can set a target deadline for its opening, and construct a calendar with a specific date of completion for each successive Action Step, up to the final outcome.

Using the steps generated for your outcome, establish a target deadline for completion of each Action Step.

Internalizing the Process

Internalizing the process means becoming so familiar with your tasks and goals for each step of the *Creaction* plan, that you no longer have to consciously think about them. Instead, your problem-solving system automatically begins to lead you down the action path to the Winner's Circle.

The expert problem-solvers who achieve complex outcomes do so because they have spent a lot of their time consciously planning and implementing their goals. Now, their process has become habitual. Automating the *Creaction* plan process is similar to learning to drive a car. At first, each function the driver performs, such as braking, steering, and accelerating, seems like a separate discrete task. Over time, and with practice, the driving becomes smooth and automatic.

As in learning to drive a car, if you continue to concretize steps in the *Creaction* plan, you will achieve a smoothly integrated and effective action performance. In the experience of most expert creative-problem-solvers, the best Internalization strategy is to practice and rehearse each part of the plan, planting reminders around the house and workplace.

In establishing a Community Youth Center, a community organizer can review the Action Steps each night so he/she will arise ready for the day. To practice, mentally review your own tasks and goals for each step along the action path toward your final outcome.

Overcoming Obstacles

Many obstacles must be overcome in proceeding with your action plan. Common obstacles include resistance from others; lack of personal resources such as motivation, initiative and ideas; and practical problems such as money, time, and locale.

To overcome resistance from others, one strategy is to organize a list of benefits for the plan, emphasizing mutual concerns with others. In planning a Community Youth Center, a creative community board member can meet with a parent/teacher association group and discuss after-school job positions for faculty and parents, extended day supervision of children with working parents, weekend family programs, and free tutoring in academic subjects for students.

Another strategy for Overcoming Obstacles is to learn personal influencing skills to help you recognize other people's cognitive and behavioral patterns. Once you recognize a pattern, you can match it, and lead others to your outcome, or you can find another way to influence the person's pattern.

To overcome the lack of personal resources and deal with practical problems, it becomes imperative that you break old habits which are interfering with your "moving on." Ask, "Why do I find it so difficult to move ahead with this plan?" List the reasons that surface. For example, "It's difficult for me to plan a Community Youth Center be-

cause..."
a.) I won't see my family enough during the organization of the center. The project will be too time-consuming.
b.) Where will I get the money? Where will I locate the center?
c.) It's really too complex a task for me to undertake by myself.

Once the list is constructed, try to blockbust each item by changing it to a new, more acceptable behavior challenge. For example, concerning item a, planning of the center can be reframed into a test of your family's patience and understanding. For b and c, planning the center can lead to acquiring new skills involving delegation of responsibility and coordinating a staff. You can become a community organizer and meet experts in the fields of grant monies, fund raising, real estate, design, and public relations.

To practice, list obstacles you may encounter for the outcome used to generate your Action Steps. How can you blockbust each of these obstacles?

Necessity Thinking

In this strategy, contrast Necessity Thinking with possibility thinking. In possibility thinking, ideas are flowing, possibilities are open, the sky is the limit. Necessity Thinking is more like "getting down to brass tacks." It is practical thinking—no "pie in the sky" pipedreams.

Why is Necessity Thinking so important in the *Creaction* phase of the **Creativity Game**? The answer is obvious—to achieve one's outcomes in reality, one must deal with reality, not fantasy. More projects have gone awry, because they were not practical or thought through carefully.

A good strategy for using Necessity Thinking is to ask, "What must really happen each step of the way for me to continue on the action path?" In contrast, a sure-fire way to insure outcome failure is to say, "Everything will work out fine, I don't have to be concerned with the details."

With respect to the Community Youth Center, Necessity Thinking leads to such questions as, "What would happen in reality if I couldn't find funding for the center?" "What will happen if community leaders don't support the project?" "What do I need to do, or learn, to gain support?"

At this time, engage in Necessity Thinking about one of your outcomes. How realistic is it? What reality tests do you need in order to know whether or not to continue down the action path?

_____

_____

_____

_____

Application of Idea-Implementation (Creaction) Strategies to Your Life Design Grid Outcomes

Now it's time to move down the action path toward the Winner's Circle. Select an outcome you recorded on the **Life Design Grid** from the Community area, and apply each *Creaction* strategy to your goal. Record your outcome and application work on the **Idea-Implementation Chart** on the next page.

Idea-Implementation Chart

Creaction
Strategy:

Outcome: _____

_____

Chunking (list major chunks)	
Risk Factors (list major risks)	
Evaluation (evaluate & list any changes in your action plan)	
Action Steps (list action steps in sequence)	
Concretizing (write a con-crete result for each action step	
Timing (determine a deadline for each action step)	
Internalizing Process (continue re-viewing this chart)	

Continued on next page

Overcoming Obstacles (list blocks & blockbusters	
Necessity Thinking (ask what would happen in reality if an action step could not be completed)	

Imagine completing action plans and taking Action Steps for all the outcomes on your **Life Design Grid**! When a balance of outcomes in your life areas of Connections, Productivity, and Self-Health is achieved, you will find yourself in the Winner's Circle.

CHAPTER EIGHT

Congratulations, Problem Solved: Connections, Productivity, and Self-Health

By now, it is hoped that you have begun to carry out many of your life design outcomes from the Connections, Productivity and Self-Health life areas. Can you imagine yourself standing in the Winner's Circle, having achieved your desired outcomes? Can you feel the glow of satisfaction that comes with a job well done—a problem carried to a successful conclusion? Can you sense the rush of exhilaration or the quiet flow of contentment that follows on the heels of victory? Can you see the gold ribbon, the trophy, that is given to those who enter the Winner's Circle? Can you hear the roar of the crowd's applause and the small voice inside you whispering, "I did it! I did it!"?

Remember that once creative-problem-solvers have tasted the fruits of the Winner's Circle, they want to return again and again. There is no end to the **Creativity Game** process in the sense that there is no end to the number of outcomes you can achieve when you let yourself be open to new and different possibilities. Creative-problem-solving is a continuous process—the more you play the **Creativity Game** the easier it becomes to eliminate obstacles, generate fresh approaches in all areas of life, and revisit the Winner's Circle.

As you practiced the **Creativity Game** in this book, you were presented with many examples of varied problems and solutions to personal, family, community, and global situations. Hopefully, you have become even more open to the alternatives which can become successful solutions in your life, and you have decided not to impose too many restrictions and limits on your choices.

When you allow yourself to be open to the expansiveness of the question, "What is possible here?", the options may lead to *change. Change* can be unsettling to both yourself and those around you. Frequently the response to *change* is, "That's an interesting idea (or solution), but it's too 'far out' for me. People will think I'm weird!" If fear of *change* is a problem for you, perhaps you should *change* your anxiety into the excitement of a challenge and ask yourself, "How can I accept *change* so my life will be richer and more satisfying, while I manage the uneasiness associated with *change?* Then, replay the **Creativity Game** and move toward the Winner's Circle, having secured the outcome of safe and satisfying *change.*

Once you have learned to accommodate *change* and can begin to accept novel and interesting solutions for your problems, give others in your life time to "come around" to accepting your novel solutions. Frequently, going with your creative flow can differ considerably from carrying on with your normal routine. Others may not feel comfortable with your new patterns. However, if it feels right for you, "go with it," teaching those significant others to flow along if possible.

As an example of going with the creative flow, one expert couple of players decided to get married in a unique fashion. A major outcome for this couple was to have all of their celebrants (family, friends, and acquaintances) feel comfortable and have maximum participation at the ceremony. Since they each had acquired a "motley crew" of connections over the years, they decided that they would have 7 ceremonies over one weekend to achieve their goals! They scheduled Buddhist, Taoist, Christian, Sufi, Native American, Jewish, and New Age ceremonies, each performed by representatives of the various denominations. They mailed computer print-out sheets and asked their guests to choose which ceremony and marriage celebration they would feel most comfortable attending. The couple suggested that the most appropriate gifts would be those which everyone could experience during the celebrations, such as food, drink, flowers, decorations, music, speeches, and love!

At first, this may sound strange. But ask yourself "Why?" Your answer would most likely be something to the effect that it's different from the "normal" way people get married. But, think about the positives of such an undertaking—the mutual planning by this couple for their matrimonial event, the pleasure of the company in experiencing a ceremony with which they're comfortable, and the interesting component of multiple joining celebrations for this newly united pair!

From this example, notice that once creativity gets its foot in the door, any number of possibilities begin to open. When you unlock the closed set of alternatives, you find that new and exciting ideas begin to escape.

To help you open your own creativity door, so you can step toward a balanced set of life satisfaction outcomes, here are *six keys* to the Winner's Circle. Each key unlocks a part of your creative-problem-solving potential. Place them together on a special key ring and let that be a symbol of your own creative-problem-solving style.

The *six keys* are:
- Envisioning your future outcomes.
- Committing yourself to "going for it."
- **GRASP**ing the essence of your problem situation.
- **FIND**ing **IDEAS** for your problem situation.
- Selecting the **BEST PICKS** for your problem situation.
- Implementing your **CREACTION** plan.

It is anticipated that you will get as keyed up over this process as avid **Creativity Game** players do. To entice you to replay the game and repeatedly stroll along the action path, some success stories of seasoned creative-problem-solving players are described on the following page.

Whenever one creative-problem-solver, a special education teacher, sees a troublesome or uncomfortable *Connections* situation brewing, she activates her interpersonal creativity stragtegy which she developed while practicing the **Creativity Game**. She says to herself silently, "TROUBLE," then sees a brightly-colored neon sign flashing, "BE CREATIVE! BE CREATIVE!" on her internal screen. Next, she mentally constructs movies of possible scenarios leading to solutions to the problem. She tests for feelings, and then acts out in reality the scenario that seems to fit best. This problem solver became aware that she had become a champion of the Winner's Circle when her creative strategy consistently led to elegant and functional solutions.

As a specific example of how she applied this strategy, this special education player noticed that her teaching assistant was not doing his share of the work. She said to herself, "TROUBLE," and her internal "BE CREATIVE" sign flashed on. Then, she began to view inwardly possible scenarios representing solutions. The scenario which felt best was one in which she matched her teaching assistant's posture, voice, eye movements, and so on, so he felt as if he had a "comrade." When they were in exquisite rapport, she began to suggest subtly what needed to be done. Soon, she saw him busily moving about the room, completing his tasks. She then *creacted* in reality this scenario and soon found herself in the Winner's Circle. Another round of the **Creativity Game** process well-played!

Another creative-problem-solver wanted to overcome a fear of public speaking to present his views on important *Global* issues. He was so successful in replaying the **Creativity Game** process, that he now travels on the international circuit implementing planetary congresses.

A third individual wanted to spread the idea of the **Creativity Game** to children in his *Community*. So, he ran workshops in the public library for children wanting to create their own games. This player used the **Creativity Game** to help each child in the workshop to create his or her own board game, complete with rules and prizes. By the end of each series, not only had this exceptional player reached the Winner's Circle, but he had brought all the children players along with him. Imagine the glow he experienced!

A fourth creative solution finder took "life extension" as a personal challenge. He went about researching and experimenting with the problem of *Self-Health* to discover the keys to longevity. His studies took him to the worlds of biology, chemistry, diet, and exercise. He examined the lives of those who had lived beyond the normal life span to discover their secrets. He is writing his second book on the topic, and while it is still too early to declare total victory over extending his life span, he has revisited the Winner's Circle again and again by uncovering and sharing the principles of longevity with his readers.

Other well-practiced players, over the years, have developed a week-long Creativity Institute[4] as part of their *Productivity* outcome. Beginning and advanced players come once a year to share their creative processes, entertain and facilitate each other through workshops, and get refueled for the next year of creative breakthroughs back home. Can you imagine a whole week of basking in the Winner's Circle with fellow players? Many of the C.P.S.I. regulars have become so attached to their yearly return that it has become an eagerly anticipated "home base" for them.

And finally, one practical champion, formerly a methodical, orderly, and dull fellow, has continued his daily routines while using the **Creativity Game** process to transform each routine into a creative challenge. He has given himself the daily task of living each routine in a novel, yet useful, way, feeling the zest of creative living while changing only the "how" of his routines, rather than the "what." For example, he has turned visiting the supermarket into a

---

[4]Creative Problem-Solving Institute held annually in June in Buffalo, New York, sponsored by the Creative Education Foundation.

memory game. As he strolls through the aisles, he notices the prices of each item he places in his shopping cart. When he reaches the check-out, he tries to guess the price as each item is unloaded, and before it is rung up. In this way, he improves his memory, increases his emotional *Self-Health*, while at the same time, checks on the accuracy of the check-out tabulation process.

In closing, you are invited to imagine what the world would be like if all its players rehearsed the **Creativity Game** process and achieved their desires for satisfying Connections, increased Productivity and emotional and physical Self-Health. What would such a world look, feel, and sound like? How would you know when you had arrived at such a world? What kind of a CREACTION PLAN would each planetary citizen have to generate to reach this common goal, and all step into the Winner's Circle together?

Many global game players share the vision of a peaceful and cooperative world. "Earthrun," a world-wide running event planned for 1986, in which torches will be carried around the globe (spreading the light), is only one example of a group of players' efforts and contributions to this global plan.

At whatever level you choose to play the **Creativity Game**—personal, family, community, or global—allow yourself to enjoy the *means*—the process of getting there, as well as the *ends*—the achievement of a balanced set of life outcomes. The more you practice playing the **Creativity Game**, the more you will come to believe in your ability to achieve your outcomes, and the more you believe in your ability, the more outcomes you are likely to achieve.

Albrecht, K. *Brain power.* NJ: Prentice Hall, 1980.

Bach, R. *New Realities Magazine,* 1984 (November-December).

Cohen, H. *You can negotiate anything.* NJ: L. Stuart, 1980.

Grayson, C. J. Jr. Networking. *The Futurist,* 1984 (June), 16-17.

Khatena, J. & Torrance, E. P. *Thinking creatively with sounds and words: Norms-technical manual.* Bensonville, IL: Scholastic Testing Service, 1981.

Kramer, D. & Bayern, C. The effects of behavioral strategies on creativity training. *The Journal of Creative Behavior,* 1984, *18(1),* 23-24.

Miller, G. The magical number seven plus or minus two...Some limits on our capacity for processing information. *Psychological Review,* 1956, *63,* 81-97.

Myers, R. E. & Torrance, E. P. *Can you imagine?* Lexington, MA: Ginn, 1965.

Osborn, A. F. *Applied imagination.* NYC: Charles Scribners, 1953.

Ostrander, S. & Schroeder, L. *Superlearning.* NYC: Dell, 1970.

Seligman, M. E. P. *Learned helplessness and depression in animals and humans.* Morristown, NJ: General Learning Press, 1976.

Whiting, C. S. *Creative thinking.* NYC: Reinhold Publishing, 1958.

Life Design Grid

	Connections	Productivity	Self-Health
Personal	S** H: F:	S: H: F:	S: H: F:
Family	S: H: F:	S: H: F:	S: H: F:
Community	S: H: F:	S: H: F:	S: H: F:
Global	S: H: F:	S: H: F:	S: H: F:

** S: – what you will *See* when your outcome is reached
  H: – what you will *Hear* when your outcome is reached
  F: – what you will *Feel* when your outcome is reached

Life Design Grid

	Connections	Productivity	Self-Health
Personal	S** H: F:	S: H: F:	S: H: F:
Family	S: H: F:	S: H: F:	S: H: F:
Community	S: H: F:	S: H: F:	S: H: F:
Global	S: H: F:	S: H: F:	S: H: F:

** S: — what you will *See* when your outcome is reached
H: — what you will *Hear* when your outcome is reached
F: — what you will *Feel* when your outcome is reached